COLONIAL
FOOD

Ann Chandonnet

SHIRE PUBLICATIONS

Published in Great Britain in 2013 by Shire Publications Ltd, Midland House, West Way, Botley, Oxford OX2 0PH, United Kingdom.

43-01 21st Street, Suite 220B, Long Island City, NY 11101, USA.

E-mail: shire@shirebooks.co.uk   www.shirebooks.co.uk

A CIP catalog record for this book is available from the British Library.

Shire Library no. 742.   ISBN-13: 978 0 74781 240 1

Ann Chandonnet has asserted her right under the Copyright, Designs and Patents Act, 1988, to be identified as the author of this book.

Designed by Tony Truscott Designs, Sussex, UK and typeset in Perpetua and Gill Sans.

Printed in China through Worldprint Ltd.

13 14 15 16 17   10 9 8 7 6 5 4 3 2 1

COVER IMAGE

The average New World settler dined on porridge or stew. The splendid table shown here features pumpkin pie, bread of several sorts, roast chicken surrounded by Lady apples, squashes, and colorful ears of Indian corn. A feast like this would be typical of a plantation or a fine restaurant in Colonial Williamsburg. (Alamy images)

TITLE PAGE IMAGE

Dried "britches beans" hang both to the right and the left of the cobblestone fireplace in this colonial cabin in Tennessee. Beside the hearth is a low chopping block, made from a stump. On the table is a wooden dough-rising bowl.

CONTENTS PAGE IMAGE

The kitchen of the Ximenez House in St. Augustine, Florida, was well equipped for elegant meals. The table holds a spice box with six lidded compartments. Sugar nippers were used to "bite" sweet bits from the hard, white cone (the form in which sugar was sold until the early nineteenth century). The Ximenez-Fatio House is owned by The National Society of the Colonial Dames in the State of Florida.

ACKNOWLEDGEMENTS

The recipe for Shepherd's Pie is courtesy Colonial Williamsburg.

Thanks to Karin Goldstein and Kathleen Wall for consulting on the text concerning Plimoth Plantation.

PHOTO ACKNOWLEDGEMENTS

I would like to thank the sites and people who have allowed me to use illustrations, which are acknowledged as follows:

Duncan Sawyer, pages 3, 65; Dennis Flynn, pages 57–8; Don Winter (front cover); Historic St. Mary's City, pages 1, 6, 14; Mount Vernon Ladies' Association, page 61; Peter Newark's Historical Pictures, pages 15, 19, 30, 75; Plimoth Plantation, pages 42, 63, 72. The illustration of the farmer sowing seed, page 57 (top), and the cook protecting her fat turkey, page 43, are from *Mother Nursery Rhymes and Tales* (1908, Philadelphia, Henry Altemus Company). The illustration of the child in a sickbed is from *Nursery Tales: A Collection of Old Favorites* (1910, Chicago, W. B. Conkey Company). All other illustrations are courtesy Fernand L. Chandonnet.

Shire Publications is supporting the Woodland Trust, the UK's leading woodland conservation charity, by funding the dedication of trees.

CONTENTS

INTRODUCTION

COLONIAL FOOD is an introduction to the extraordinary culinary transformation kindled when explorers and colonists from England, Europe and Russia arrived in North America. Their challenge was to survive in the New World and prepare previously unknown foods like maize, potatoes, tomatoes, chocolate and chilies. Colonial diet was shaped by Old World habits, and seeds brought from home, as well as plants harvested in the wild and crops cultivated by Native Americans. American staples like corn (maize), various squashes and beans were quickly accepted by newcomers.

Preparing colonial food was not simply a matter of making new ingredients palatable. It also required a staggering range of skills: chopping kindling, keeping a fire burning indefinitely, plucking feathers from fowl, butchering animals large and small, cosseting bread yeast, brewing beer, making cheese, adjusting "burners" of coals on a hearth and gauging the temperature of a bake oven. There were related skills, too, such as milking, making soap and candles, grinding corn, fermenting vinegar, pulverizing sugar, drying damp flour and recycling stale bread.

The housewife's universe spiraled out from hearth and barnyard to tending a kitchen garden and perhaps a large vegetable garden, as well as assisting with the grain harvest. Growing and processing flax and hemp might have been counted among her endless chores.

Preserving methods were limited to drying, smoking, pickling and salting, so the cold months of the year saw a more limited diet than warm months. Dried apples and pumpkin were important staples, while sauerkraut and root vegetables like turnips were common winter fare.

In the seventeenth century, the ordinary frontiersman dined chiefly on corn, or "Indian", in some form—hoe cake, samp, hominy or Hasty Pudding. Ben Franklin discussed the delights of Indian in two essays. Corn's flavor, he enthused, "is one of the most agreeable and wholesome ... in the world; that its green ears roasted are a delicacy beyond expression; that samp, hominy, succatash, and nokehock, made of it, are so many pleasing varieties."

Opposite:
On a bed of stewed greens, roast chicken blanketed with gravy takes center place for dinner, surrounded by individual vegetable fritters. Bread, baked in a clay casserole, has already been sampled.

Samp was a porridge made from beaten or boiled corn. Hominy (from the Algonquian *rockahominy*) is dry corn with the hull and germ removed, often coarsely ground as in hominy grits. Succatash or succotash (from the Narragansett *msickquatash*, boiled whole corn kernels) is corn mixed with beans, sometimes enriched with fish. Nokehock was parched corn cooked in hot ashes, then pounded into meal.

Cornmeal mush was seasoned with pork, small game, greens, or pumpkin. Typical meals were mush with cream, oatmeal dumplings and gravy, barley broth, or fried sausage with roasted sweet potatoes. However by the eighteenth century, on thriving plantations and in Virginia's colonial capital, Williamsburg, European-trained cooks held sway. Hence, diners grew accustomed to fish in pastry, venison pie, ragout of cucumbers, fried ox tongue and imported tipples.

A nice white gravy over a simple boiled chicken was no longer sufficient for entertaining. The goal was to set a table comparable to London's best. Among the gentry, hostesses spared no expense.

An open door admits sunlight to a cabin's main room. A rope bed takes up one corner. Living, cooking and sleeping in a common space was typical of the seventeenth century.

Above: The Indian corn found by the Pilgrims was various colors, including yellow, blue and red. Each ear bore just eight rows of kernels. After four centuries of horticultural improvement, today's ear has nearly double that.

Left: To preserve them for winter eating, rings of squash dry over an open fire. Photographed at Hart's Square, a privately owned colonial village near Hickory, North Carolina.

Below: In this Tennessee cabin's fireplace, a wall-mounted swinging iron crane supports a large pot ready for cooking—eliminating the danger of stepping into the fireplace. Three cast-iron skillets hang within easy reach.

ARRIVING IN THE
NEW WORLD

AFTER Christopher Columbus proved that there was desirable land on the far side of the Atlantic in the last years of the fifteenth century, European countries strove for empire. With guile, enslavement, smallpox and genocide,

By window light, an interpreter in period costume prepares vegetables and fruits including onions and apples for a seventeenth-century feast in Maryland. Dried garlic flanks the window.

Columbus conquered the Arawak of the Bahamas, Cortés the Aztecs of Mexico and Pizarro the Incas of Peru.

In Alta California and other Spanish colonies, missionaries employed Native Americans to cultivate crops including figs, lemons and oranges.

To encourage colonists the British published a prospectus in 1588, Thomas Harriot's *A Brief and True Report of the New Found Land of Virginia*. Harriot gamely sampled "the victuall of the country, of which some forms were very straunge unto us." He mentions provender already known—such as corn—but adds others: sassafras, sunflowers, medlar, and sturgeon.

As explorers feverishly pursued precious metals, tasty, nourishing new foods were an afterthought. Columbus, however, had an inkling of their worth. He wrote in his diary: "There are trees of a thousand kinds all producing their own kind of fruit, and all wonderfully aromatic; I am the saddest man in the world at not recognizing them, because I am certain that they are all of value."

When England established Jamestown in 1608, gold was still the prime mover. Grumbling bellies interfered. When Captain John Smith explored with forty-six men, fierce weather stranded his party at an Indian town. Thus Smith kept Christmas "among the Salvages, where we were never more merry, nor fed on more plentie of good Oysters, Fish, Flesh, Wild-foule, and

The curve of land today known as Cape Cod was named "Port du Cap" by Samuel de Champlain in 1606. This map, possibly drawn by Champlain himself, shows Native American dwellings surrounded by corn fields. It was published in *Les Voyages du Sieur de Champlain*, Paris, 1613.

good bread; nor never had better fires in England than in the dry smoky houses of Kecoughtan."

In Canada, British and French vied for rule with Native Americans and each other over several centuries. First John Cabot (in 1497), explored the coast, followed by Martin Frobisher in 1576. French explorers were Jacques Cartier (1534) and Samuel de Champlain (1603). In the Huron longhouses, Champlain shared dog flesh and *sagamite*—a concoction of dried corn and *migan*, a mixture of cornmeal and smoked fish. The first colonists were French, settling at Port Royal in 1605 and at Quebec City in 1608. The French in seventeenth-century Nova Scotia subsisted on wheat, barley and oats plus garden vegetables, supplemented by livestock, game and fish. Eel stew was a favorite fall dish. Quebec's Algonquin introduced colonists to foods such as maple syrup, butternuts and moose.

In 1609, Henry Hudson and the *Half Moon* entered Hudson River proper. Exploring, the crew passed an outcropping of the Catskills and encountered the Mahicans. A local elder welcomed Hudson with a feast of pigeon and fat dog.

Settlements like Plimoth were inspired by Old World religious persecution. Although the square-rigged merchantman *Mayflower* was originally headed for Hudson's River, it anchored off New England in December 1620. Anxious to transfer provisions to shore, the 102 colonists chose a site they named Plimoth and speedily framed a 20-foot-square post-and-beam shelter. Meals were cooked over open fires. In the spring, wattle and daub houses rose in two parallel defensive rows. In these rude, one-room dwellings, kettles suspended in open hearths served to heat water and see the (cook at a low boil) meat and vegetables. Fireplaces also offered the possibility of roasting food.

GIVING THANKS

On the *Mayflower*, the Pilgrims carried hardtack, beer, butter, lemons, sugar, eggs, smoked bacon and herring, oatmeal, dried peas and beans, salted cod, and hard cheese. As staples ran short, meals became dreary rounds of mush and pease porridge.

When most Americans think of Thanksgiving, they date it to the fall of 1621, to a celebration

Wattle and daub construction was common across Europe in Neolithic times and continued to be employed in the colonies, especially for smokehouses, stables, tool sheds, corncribs, well houses and chicken coops. Photographed at the Schiele Museum's Backcountry Farm.

held by Pilgrims at New Plimoth. However, North America had long hosted feasts of thanksgiving, many of them Native American. British fishermen gave thanks for the bounty of codfish and whales in 1578 in Newfoundland. And in 1607 came a prayerful observance at Sir John Popham's Colony on Maine's Kennebec River.

To promote drying and keeping, squares of hardtack are pierced with a ten-penny nail before going into the oven.

On his first explorations of the territory around Plimoth in 1620, Edward Winslow found strawberry plants, sorrel, wild onions and maize. The following day his shore party dined on ducks and fat geese. A Londoner who arrived on the ship *Fortune* in 1621 wrote glowingly of "the great store of fruits ... walnuts, chestnuts, small nuts and plums ... much variety of flowers, roots and herbs ... turkeys, quail, pigeon, partridges, fish, fowls, beaver and otters." *Mourt's Relation*, penned mostly by Winslow, gives more details about the local foods available.

The First Thanksgiving 1621, a romanticized view of grateful Pilgrims and their Native American neighbors sharing food. Painting by Jean Leon Gerome Ferris, c. 1915.

CRANBERRY BEANS WITH SAGE

2 pounds fresh cranberry (also known as shell, pinto, barlotti) beans, weight in pods

salt to taste

3 tablespoons olive oil or bacon fat

½ teaspoon dried sage

Shell beans and cook them until tender in water just to cover. Allow all the water to cook away. Heat oil in a frying pan and add beans. Add seasonings, and cover. Cook until all the oil is absorbed, shaking the pan from time to time to keep the beans from sticking or burning. Six servings.

When the Pilgrims laid plans for an autumnal celebration, perhaps they had in mind the ancient secular British festival of Harvest Home—a time of revelry, sports and feasting; or, in the spirit of freedom of choice, Powder Plot Day, celebrated on November 5. Available for the meal would have been ruffed grouse, passenger pigeon, nuts, clams and juniper berries.

Of 1621, *Mourt's Relation* reports, "Our harvest being gotten in, our governor sent four men on fowling, that so we might after a special manner rejoice together after we had gathered the fruit of our labors. They four in one day killed as much fowl as, with a little help beside, served the company almost a week." Massasoit, leader of the Pokanoket group of the Wampanoag, attended the Pilgrims' Thanksgiving with ninety followers. His warriors contributed five deer to the feast.

The menu that first Thanksgiving perhaps included cranberry beans with sage, stewed pumpkin, corn pones, spit-roasted venison with vinegar-herb sauce, stewed squash, succotash, goose, duck, turkey and pigeon fricassee.

The flower of rattlesnake bean, a type of shell bean whose green stage may be eaten as a string bean, glows on a vine climbing up a stalk of Indian corn.

In Quebec in 1639, two Ursuline nuns and three members of the Hospitalières order established a hospital and school. Eight Huron girls were accepted as pupils at the school. When the girls' parents visited, they were entertained with a stew combining a bushel of black plums, 24 pounds of bread, large measures of Indian corn and ground-peas, a dozen melted tallow candles and 2 or 3 pounds of salt pork.

France chose Pierre Le Moyne, a native of the Montreal colony, to lead the colonization of Louisiana. Early in 1699, a fort was constructed

Spanish and Portuguese ships headed for the New World stocked up on live pigs at the Canary Islands. Some of these animals escaped on Georgia's Ossabaw Island. Their descendants are known as Ossaba pigs.

on Biloxi Bay, but intense heat killed crops, and garrison discipline was lax. French colonists in Louisiana and Mississippi grew cash crops like tobacco, indigo and rice.

Hungry for rumored cities of gold, the Spanish dispatched expeditions to Mexico and Peru, and north from Florida as far as the Carolinas. From the Cherokees they learned of corncob jelly, yam cakes, and hickory nut milk (*ganu gwala sti*). The newcomers introduced cabbage, lemons, cucumbers, figs, garlic, lettuce, oranges, peaches, sugarcane and wheat, plus swine and sheep.

NEW FOODS

The ancient grains chia, amaranth and quinoa were staples in the Pre-Columbian diet. Images of corn cobs adorn their decorative pottery. Conquistadors invading Peru found Incan sun priestesses wearing sunflower crowns and gold sunflowers adorning temples to honor the sun god. Chocolate was buried with the dead and used to anoint newborns.

The Inca used mortars of volcanic rock to grind chili peppers, avocado, roasted cocoa seeds and dried corn kernels. Each hand-carved *molcajete* has three legs—believed to pay homage to the god of the hearth, Huehueteotl.

The conquerors dismissed the value of Mesoamerican cultures. Spanish Bishop Diego de Landa gave orders in 1562 for the burning of at least forty Mayan codices, which he judged full of "superstition and the Devil's falsehoods." Foods linked to indigenous religion were banned,

QUINOA
 1 cup uncooked quinoa
 2 cups water or stock
Place quinoa in a fine sieve, and place sieve over a large bowl. Cover quinoa with water. With your hands, rub the grains together for 30 seconds; rinse and repeat. Drain well. Combine quinoa with water and salt to taste in a medium saucepan. Bring to a boil. Reduce heat and simmer for 15 minutes or until water is absorbed. Fluff with a fork. Mild in flavor, this pseudo-cereal is high in protein and low in fat.

The European granary building, common since Neolithic times, was recycled in the colonies as a corncrib, as in this example at Colonial Williamsburg.

and the Inca were forced to grow wheat instead. Thus began the conquistadors' broad influence on world diet. They introduced onions and rice to Peru at the beginning of the sixteenth century. To Europe they carried a wealth of American foods: tomatoes, roasted pumpkin seeds, chili peppers, sweet (bell) peppers, chocolate and potatoes.

On four voyages to the New World, Columbus sought spices and slaves; he found haricot beans, yuca, cassava, guava, papaya and Taino barbecue (*barbacoa*). In the West Indies alone, he was introduced to pineapple, sweet potatoes and corn. Within fifty years of their arrival, the Spanish had established plantations in the West Indies, Mexico and other locations, and the foods Columbus had discovered were being planted as far away as China.

The "good bread" savored by Captain John Smith was likely oval cornmeal pones (small, oval loaves). Europeans took to corn with a will. Colonial families often consumed it three times a day.

Rice (*Oryza sativa*) was another new food—traveling *into* the Americas. Cultivated in India since 3000 BC, this member of the grass family was introduced to Holland's West African colonies in the fifteenth century. It reached North America at the end of the seventeenth century. Africans familiar with rice cultivation were brought as slaves to southern colonies to establish rice plantations.

Certain American foods completely new to Europeans were so easy to harvest that they were doomed. The Eastern bison, for instance, was extinct by 1825. This large, dark bison bore a smaller hump than its Plains cousin and

The Catawba Nation "town hall" was a large building used exclusively for ceremonies and entertaining guests.

A well-fed and obviously prosperous German immigrant farmer from Pennsylvania, c. 1750, decorates the top of an oval wooden box.

Three costumed interpreters cook a meal over an open fire in the seventeenth-century manner. A wooden tripod supports the heavy iron kettle.

ranged from Canada to Georgia. Many bison were slaughtered for their tongues alone, which were considered choice delicacies.

The passenger pigeon was another victim of colonial appetite. This forest dweller had a range extending from Canada and the Great Lakes to the Great Plains and south to Virginia. Swedish taxonomist Pehr Kahm described its splendid migration in March 1749: "There came from the north an incredible multitude of these pigeons to Pennsylvania and New Jersey. Their number, in flight, extended three or four English miles in length ... and they flew so closely together that the sky and the sun were obscured..." Close formations made it easy to bring down a dozen with one shotgun blast. By 1850 these slim fowl were nearing extinction. Similarly, sleeping doves could easily be knocked from their perches with a stick.

On the other hand, the beautiful wild turkey, a fowl new to colonists, survived. Mayans in the Yucatan introduced the showy bird to Cortés in 1519. The Dutch lawyer and landowner Adriaen Van der Donck put this fine fowl at 20 to 30 pounds.

Combining new foods with Old World foods yielded countless savory dishes in what would today be called "fusion cuisine": dishes including pumpkin custard and cod chowder, both made with cow's milk; and the Spanish dish paella, combining New World tomatoes with Old World seafood and rice.

NATIVE AMERICAN INFLUENCES

Native Americans began dabbling in agriculture about 8,000 years ago with the nutritious sunflower. Farming began about 2,500 years ago—chiefly in fertile bottomland. A thousand years ago, the Pre-Columbian "three sisters"—corn, beans and squash—were being traded north and east from the Rio Grande. In the Mississippi Valley, gardeners domesticated such plants as marsh elder and lamb's-quarters in the 1500s.

As the Pilgrims raided empty summer residences or villages emptied by disease to gather the stored foodstuffs, as Jamestown residents observed Chesapeake Indians, and the North Carolina frontiersmen supped with Cherokee acquaintances, they encountered appetizing new foods. Corn, beans and squash were the main sustenance of eastern tribes, and the colonists quickly adopted them. Turn-about was fair play; colonists introduced Indians to metheglin—their version of mead, seasoned with mint, rosemary and burnet.

New Englanders depended on pumpkin as much as they did on corn. "Let no man make a jest at Pumpkins," wrote chronicler Edward Johnson in 1654, "for with this fruit

Native to the Americas, sunflowers have been prized by Native Americans for 8,000 years. Meal from seeds enriched bread and thickened stews. Sunflower seed oil served to groom hair and to treat snakebite and heatstroke.

the Lord was pleased to feed his people to their good content, till Corne [i.e. grain] and Cattell were increased." Pumpkin even became beer, immortalized in the couplet: "Oh we can make liquor to sweeten our lips / Of pumpkins, of parsnips, of walnut-tree chips."

When Europeans settled Pennsylvania, they learned from local tribes about native medicinal herbs as well as butternuts and red oak acorns. Pennsylvania tribes cultivated corn, knotweed and lamb's-quarters. A Chickasaw soup of beans and hominy proved a colonial favorite.

Louisiana was home to crawfish, filé (powdered root bark of the small tree known as sassafras) and pecans. The Choctaw of Louisiana, Alabama

Native Americans from New England to the Carolinas continued to reside in bark-covered housing until the eighteenth century, when log homes prevailed. Photographed at Hart's Square.

and Mississippi developed *banaha*, a pease porridge with cornmeal. Wrapped in corn husks, the thick mixture was boiled to produce a variant on the tamale (cornmeal dough wrapped around a filling, then enclosed in corn husks and steamed). As the Spanish introduced pigs, the adaptable Choctaw invented *tash-labona*, combining pork with cracked corn.

Considering these influences, one sees how cuisines have washed back and forth over one another like waves on a fertile shore. As Jack Weatherford wrote in *Indian Givers: How the Indians of the Americas Transformed the World*, "Sichuan beef with chiles, German chocolate cake, curried potatoes, vanilla ice cream, Hungarian goulash, peanut brittle, and pizza all owe their primary flavorings to the American Indians."

Lamb's-quarters, a wild relative of spinach, was cultivated by Native Americans. The floury young leaves are cooked like spinach. Navajos used the dried seeds in bread and pancakes.

A colonial family harvesting corn. The housewife has brought her infant along for the day's work in the fields, cradling the babe in a tree.

FARMING IN THE EARLY COLONIES

Deep in autumn leaves, a lane enclosed with "worm" fence leads to a group of colonial cabins at the Museum of Appalachia.

W HEN European colonists arrived in the New World, their attempts at agriculture were impeded by the dense forest spreading from the Atlantic to the Mississippi. Immense trees prevented sunlight from reaching the ground. Thus, colonial farming commenced with an axe. Clearing was a matter of felling trees, burning brush, and waiting for obdurate stumps to loosen sufficiently to be pulled from their sockets like rotten teeth.

The laborious process took years. Gradually, tiny plots of corn and potatoes aggregated into spacious pastures and fields.

At Jamestown, with no gold in sight, food was earned with the sweat of the brow, employing hoe, spade and mattock. Following years of drought and starvation, John Rolfe suggested tobacco as a cash crop, and it became the mainstay of the region's economy for two centuries. Initially, indentured servants did the cultivation, but in 1619 slaves and plows were imported.

The Pilgrims were fortunate to inherit cleared ground from Native Americans who had perished from diseases introduced by early explorers, and there they planted their "alien corn"—an eight-row, multi-colored flint variety. In spring 1621, they planted 20 acres of maize plus 6 acres of grain and peas. Wolves and crows had to be kept

Rather than sowing in drills (rows), some colonial kitchen gardens were laid out in squares, in which precious seeds were broadcast. Photographed at the Schiele Museum, Gastonia, North Carolina.

Native Americans interplanted the "three sisters": corn, beans and squash. Corn stalks provide natural supports for bean vines like these Rattlesnake beans.

away from the herring used to manure the corn. The harvest equaled a peck per person per week. Governor William Bradford wrote, "God be praised, we had a good increase of Indian corn, and our barley indifferent good, but our peas not worth the gathering, for we fear they were too late sown."

In 1623, Bradford was persuaded that individual plots would be tilled more enthusiastically than a common one. The stratagem worked. However, drought that year forced hungry pilgrims to subsist on ground nuts and shellfish, and to barter with Natives for corn and beans. Yarrow, wild onions, lamb's-quarters, plantain, nettles, dock, liverwort, and watercress were used to supplement their diet.

By 1630, however, Reverend Francis Higginson, Salem's first pastor, could write enthusiastically: "Our turnips, parsnips and carrots are here both bitter than and sweeter than is ordinary to be found in England. Here are stores of pumpions, cucumbers, and other things of that nature... Plentie of strawberries in their time, and pennyroyall, winter saverie, carvell and water-cresses, also leeks and onions..."

In 1640, Massachusetts had 16,000 settlers and grew English wheat that was traded at the new commerce center of Boston. Orchards groaned with fruit, and by 1650 goodwives proudly served apple, pear and quince tarts.

A
RELATION OR

Iournall of the beginning and proceedings
of the English Plantation setled at *Plimoth* in N E W
E N G L A N D, by certaine English Aduenturers both
Merchants and others.

With their difficult passage, their safe ariuall, their
ioyfull building of, and comfortable planting them-
selues in the now well defended Towne
of N E W P L I M O T H.

AS ALSO A RELATION OF FOVRE

seuerall discoueries since made by some of the
same English Planters there resident.

I. In a iourney to P V C K A N O K I C K *the habitation of the Indians greatest King* Massasoyt : *as also their message, the answer and entertainment
they had of him.*

I I. In a voyage made by ten of them to the Kingdome of Nawset, *to seeke
a boy that had lost himselfe in the woods : with such accidents as befell them
in that voyage.*

I I I. In their iourney to the Kingdome of Namascnet, *in defence of their
greatest King* Massasoyt, *against the* Narrohiggonsets, *and to reuenge the
supposed death of their Interpreter* Tisquantum.

I I I I. Their voyage to the Massachusets, *and their entertainment there.*

With an answer to all such obiections as are any way made
against the lawfulnesse of English plantations
in those parts.

LONDON,

Printed for *Iohn Bellamie,* and are to be sold at his shop at the two
Greyhounds in Cornhill neere the Royall Exchange, 1622.

SEVENTEENTH-CENTURY FOOD

WHETHER MUSSELS, corn, wheat or goat, colonial food was cooked in an open hearth. Families occupied a single room, dominated by an 8-foot-wide fireplace that supplied both warmth and light. With iron scarce, the first lug poles were green wood. Inevitably the pole dried, charred and broke, depositing dinner in the ashes—begetting the expression "the fat is in the fire."

The average colonial farm or homestead was modest. The residence was generally less than 600 square feet, perhaps overlaid by a loft where children slept. As had been true for centuries, the day dawned with a simple gruel or porridge, served in wooden trenchers or gourd bowls. Hearth cooking centered on the simplest of fare—stews of beans, peas and vegetables; or a hash of leftovers. Protein sources ranged from deer to bluebirds, from raccoon to salt pork to smoked ham hocks. Breads were baked in covered cast-iron pots. Few hard-working colonists complained of the food. As Cervantes reckoned, "Hunger is the best sauce."

The typical New Netherland hearth was shallow, with a hood to carry away smoke. It was equipped with a hanging iron pot, a spit, a frying pan and several three-footed pots (*grapen*) that sat above coals. A well-equipped kitchen held a hair sieve, a nutmeg grater, a dozen pewter porringers and a bread grater.

The word "locavore" would not be coined for centuries, but all societies before the industrial revolution consumed foods seasonally. Eating what is grown or raised within a 20-mile radius is nothing new. Early colonists generally ate only what they could themselves hunt, gather or grow.

FOOD AND MEDICINE

In colonial times, food and medicine were kissing cousins. The frontier housewife served as attending physician—cooling fevers, stitching wounds, and compounding palliatives. It is understandable, then, that one of the first comprehensive reports from the New World, *Mourt's Relation*, repeatedly mentions the presence of wild sassafras in Massachusetts Bay. Root and bark compounds of this tree were valuable curatives throughout the Old World.

Opposite: Named for the G. Mourt cited in its preface, *Mourt's Relation* (1622) was the first book published about Plimoth Colony. Most of the text was written by *Mayflower* pilgrim Edward Winslow.

Two North American nuts, glossy horse chestnuts (yellow buckeyes) and sweet pecans, provide concentrated protein—horse chestnuts for pigs, squirrels and deer; pecans for humans. Native Americans processed acorns and horse chestnuts into an edible flour.

The stone floor of the kitchen prevented stray coals from starting a fire. This kitchen is separate from the planter's brick dwelling. Photographed at Oakley Plantation, St. Francisville, Louisiana, where Audubon painted some of his famous bird portraits.

Housewives learned to set bones with Algonquin splints of birch bark and to treat rheumatism with oil of wintergreen. Colonists gathered and grew roots and herbs including catnip, pennyroyal, sage, thoroughwort, spearmint, tansy and wormwood for medicinal use. Salem's Dr. Zerobabel Endecott (d. 1684) applied this preparation to a sprain: "Take stronge bere

este [yeast] & honye, of equall quantyty & boyle them to the Consistanty of honye & so apply it hott to ye place greeued." Other medicaments of the day included elk's hoof, saffron, small spiders, peony seeds, tobacco, conserve of rose petals, turmeric, and powder of wolves' guts.

The housewife brewed tisanes of basil and thyme for women in labor, borage for melancholy, chamomile for kidney stones, and comfrey for hemorrhoids. Slippery Elm tea or molasses warmed with bear fat was spooned out to soothe coughs.

FOOD FOR SLAVES

When slave ships slipped anchor at African ports like Senegal, they took aboard familiar foods like okra, eggplant and peanuts. American planters realized that their African charges yearned for these comestibles and so acquired seeds.

An apothecary's table at the Museum of Appalachia displays a bottle of cholera medicine (left) and a tincture of balsam as well as a mortar and pestle for pulverizing ingredients.

Cheap provender like cornmeal, offal meats and field greens were slave fodder. Suppers might consist of black-eyed peas (also known as pigeon peas, field peas, or crowder peas) and turnip greens seasoned with hog jowl, or sweet potatoes and buttermilk. The slave dish Buckling was based on herring preserved in brine. The headless fish were fried and served with hoe cakes or whole-wheat bread.

Between 1716 and 1762, an average of 70,000 slaves came ashore in the American colonies each year. In Alabama and other slave states, plantations could compass as many as 5,000 acres—a far cry from the average colonial homestead. At George Washington's 800-acre Virginia plantation, Mount Vernon, his first cash crop was tobacco. However, drought and poor returns encouraged a switch in 1787 to flax, hemp, cotton, silk, and wheat—all cared for by slaves.

After dosing her ill granddaughter with a home remedy such as horehound syrup, a grandmother keeps the little girl company during her illness.

Merchant and rice planter Henry Laurens of Charleston was one of the first to import eggplant to the New World, where it was used as a table ornament until the nineteenth century.

Virginia laws allowed slaves to be worked fifteen hours a day. Solomon Northup, a Louisiana plantation slave, wrote that field hands had a mere ten to fifteen minutes at noon to eat: "All that is allowed them is corn and bacon, which is given at the corncrib and smoke-house every Sunday morning. Each one receives, as his weekly allowance, three and a half pounds of bacon, and corn enough to make a peck of meal."

In the Carolinas, broken and dirty rice was doled out, and slaves gathered pokeweed (a spring green still eaten in "sallets"). Slaves sometimes raised their own food, but the majority of American planters did not allow even this leisure. Many male slaves did not consume enough protein to sustain them; however, masters found it more economical to replace slaves every two or three years than to feed them well. Indentured servants were treated just as badly—and sometimes rebelled, as did slaves.

For the master's table, the creative African-American cook melded American, European and African foods to create tasty new dishes. Peanuts, black-eyed peas, guinea hens, eggplant, spinach, okra, sesame seeds, sorghum and watermelon came from Africa. Sweet potatoes, melons, squash and beans were Native American crops. The result: sweet potato pie, watermelon rind pickle, spoonbread and gumbo—from the Bantu for okra; a savory stew of tomatoes, vegetables, seafood and chicken or ham, thickened with okra pods.

A favorite in colonies of the American South, spoonbread is a culinary descendant of the Native American corn porridge, Suppone or Suppawn. Buttery custard floats on top, with hearty "polenta" at the bottom.

FARMING IN THE EIGHTEENTH CENTURY

GENERATIONS of Americans added to what their ancestors had wrestled from the wilderness. By 1754, the German traveler Gottlieb Mittelberger could say of southeastern Pennsylvania: "Many a farmer has 50 or 100 and even 200–400 acres of land, laid out in orchards, meadows, fields, and woods."

The backwoods farmer of modest means relied on his large family for labor. He raised cotton, hemp and flax, cobbled his own shoes and constructed all his own furniture. Farms typically contained a mini-orchard: two peach trees, two plum, half a dozen apple, and one quince—valued for pectin.

Plantations were more complex than backwoods homesteads. For example, George Washington's place of residence was originally a modest farmhouse. Profits allowed him to rebuild twice on the original foundations. Eventually the grand house encompassed 7,000 square feet, with a 1,400-square foot piazza flanked by a bowling green. Outbuildings included a storehouse, smokehouse, wash house, grist mill, and stable. A small fishing fleet provided slave food and export goods.

The kitchen garden was supplemented with a greenhouse, a strawberry patch and espaliered fruit trees. Washington had high expectations: "Tell the gardener I expect everything that a Garden ought to produce, in the most ample manner," he wrote.

In 1775, a young Scottish woman, Janet Schaw, visited her brother Robert's plantation on the Cape Fear River in North Carolina. She witnessed land cleared through controlled burning and the use of worm (zigzag) fence. Schaw's *Journal of a Lady of Quality* noted what she considered inefficient tilling:

I expected to have found the fields completely ploughed at least, if not sown and harrowed; but how much was my amazement increased to find that every instrument of husbandry was unknown here; not only all the various ploughs, but all the machinery used with such success at home, and that the only

Opposite:
A painting of cultivated farmland in Pennsylvania, c. 1750, shows an orchard laid out in upper right.

Above: Peach blossom reaches for the spring sun. Christopher Columbus brought peach seeds to the New World on his second and third voyages. Franciscan monks introduced peaches to islands off Georgia in 1571.

instrument used is a hoe, with which they at once till and plant corn. To accomplish this a number of Negroes follow each other's tail the day long ... and it will take twenty at least to do as much work as two horses with a man and a boy would perform.

As a Renaissance man whose studies included horticulture, Thomas Jefferson considered agriculture "a science of the very first order." He commenced gardening at Monticello in 1770. By 1796, he owned 170 slaves, making it possible to introduce terracing in 1806. When the gardens were at their peak in 1812, the plantation cultivated more than 250 different varieties of vegetables as well as fruit trees, almond shrubs, figs, and berries in "squares." He grew marrowfat peas, zucchini, hanging onions, broccoli from Italy, salsify ("oyster plant"),

Right: Two farmers take a pair of Lineback oxen (a heritage breed) through their paces, plowing a field at a demonstration farm in Colonial Williamsburg.

okra, corn salad, endive, Tennis Ball lettuce, sesame (for salad oil) and sea kale. Exploring biodiversity with seeds imported from Paris, he was the first non-aboriginal to grow tomatoes. In about 1794, Jefferson addressed the prevention of soil erosion in Virginia's Piedmont by designing a plow specifically for hillsides.

The colonial garden at Williamsburg exemplifies a household plot. Worked entirely with hand tools and watered from an above-ground cistern, this garden produces rocket (arugula), cardoons, salsify, skirrets (a member of the parsley family with an edible root) and purple sprouting broccoli.

Above: Looking like plumes on a green hat, cardoons grow in an eighteenth-century-style garden. Of Mediterranean origin, cardoons are cousins to the artichoke; roots and leaves are eaten after blanching.

EIGHTEENTH-CENTURY FOOD

A S TIME PASSED, colonists were able to add to their dwellings. The "hall" (kitchen) became a separate room. By the early 1700s, iron cranes replaced wooden lug poles, and cooks could tend their pots without stepping into the fireplace. Kitchen equipment expanded to include tip kettles, three-legged spiders and toaster racks that held two slices of bread side-by-side.

A COLONIAL HOMESTEAD MENU
Oatmeal, Pea or Barley Porridge
Corn Lightbread
Baked Beans with Salt Pork or Bear Fat

At a colonial homestead an itinerant minister might be served a roast chicken, a "mess" of greens and sweet apple dumplings—but nothing grander. Whereas an early Plimoth dish of hare was probably hare and water, Jugged Hare in Virginia *c.* 1780 was a complicated dish of onion, hare, turnip, celery, breadcrumbs, ham, veal, currant jelly, chestnuts and suet. The imported ingredients include cloves, lemon, mace, peppercorns and port.

At plantations, dining was lavish. The Washingtons were known as gracious hosts who entertained regularly; for example, in 1768, Mount Vernon hosted eighty-two dinner parties over 291 days. Washington enjoyed showing off his improvements. In a letter dated November 23, 1794, he wrote, "I have no objection to any sober or orderly person's gratifying their curiosity in viewing the buildings, Gardens, &..." A ham was boiled daily in case of unexpected guests. Tea was laid on the piazza with views of the Potomac. Visitors like the Marquis de Lafayette were served a cake version of gingerbread—expensive due to the imported spice—but more elegant social occasions called for imports: Lucca olives, Rhenish wine, champagne and Spanish pimentos. Plates of ice cream brought gasps of approval; among the gentry, ice houses were becoming *de rigueur* by the close of the eighteenth century.

Opposite:
A potter at Old Salem spins his wheel. Salem, founded in North Carolina in 1766, was the central community in a 100,000-acre tract. It served as a hub of economic trade and Moravian spiritual life.

A trio of warm apple dumplings awaits diners.

On the dining table it was out with wood and pewter, and in with china, glittering silver and crystal. Pickles, preserves, jellies in gem-like colors, sweetmeats and relishes were displayed in elaborate corner dishes. These treats included cherries in brandy, spiced cantaloupe, orange marmalade and walnut catsup.

Haute cuisine in the French manner became the order of the day in the eighteenth century, with sauces, stocks, glazes and soufflés. Cooks in well-to-do households took time to mold dishes in fancy shapes like hen's nests, employ puff paste [pastry], stack up pyramids of ice creams and create "surprises." The simple peasant pease porridge made from dried peas and a soup bone was supplanted by Eliza Smith's elegant soup of leeks, spinach, anchovies, mint, butter, and bacon, garnished with tiny meatballs and toast points and served in an elegant tureen, naturally.

In Williamsburg, dinner at the Governor's Palace was served at 2 p.m in several courses, with a variety of meats and baked goods. Here is a possible menu:

George Washington's dining table was adorned with implements like this silver wine coaster and pewter funnel. The original of the funnel, used for decanting wine, was made about 1750 by an English pewterer. Reproductions by the Metropolitan Museum of Art.

A WILLIAMSBURG PALACE MENU
Mulligatawny Soup
Chicken Salad
Fish in Pastry
Fried Cucumbers
Corn Fritters
Carrot Pudding
Venison and Rabbit Pie
Chicken and Leek Pie
Chicken Hash
Fried Ox Tongue
Peach and Lavender Ice Cream
Wine, Brandy, Blackberry Cordial, Coffee

Dishes were heavily seasoned with herbs or costly spices like nutmeg and cinnamon. William Sparrow, head cook at the palace from 1769 to 1770, rose early to choose provisions at the market, draw up a menu, and assign duties to his assistants.

The haunting flavor of peach-lavender ice cream is created by steeping aromatic dried or fresh lavender flowers in warm cream.

Printen or "picture cookies" are also known as Speculaas or Springerle. They originated more than 500 years ago as a holiday tradition in Holland, Belgium, northern Germany and Scandinavia. The original presses were carved in clay or wood. For information about modern and reproduction cookie presses, see www.houseon thehill.net.

Special occasions demanded sumptuous fare. For example, when Britain's victory at the Battle of Culloden was celebrated in Williamsburg with a grand ball, the *Virginia Gazette* of July 18, 1746, records the supper served: "a very handsome collation spread on three Tables, in three different Rooms, consisting of near 100 Dishes..." Outside, hogsheads of punch were ladled to the populace.

For the holidays, colonists scrimped to purchase luxuries like sugar, dried currants, almonds, raisins, cinnamon and ginger. Dutch settlers baked printen, while Germans passed plates of gingerbread, quince paste and marzipan. British colonists supped upon roast beef, mince pie, eggnog, and plum pudding. In 1709, Virginia governor William Byrd II's Christmas table groaned under "turkey and chine, roast apples and wine, tongue and udder." Celebrations might last two weeks. For Christmas 1787, George Washington hired a camel to delight his guests, most of whom would never have seen one before.

DINNER AWAY FROM HOME

For diners far from home, taverns, inns or ordinaries fed and lodged travelers while simultaneously providing townspeople with a hall for socializing or celebration. In the early seventeenth century, both Connecticut and Massachusetts required that every community provide an ordinary to entertain strangers. County courts regulated prices for food, drink, lodging and stables. Constables warned landlords of habitual drunkards, who were not to be served.

Many ordinaries were located near county seats or ferry landings. Some were little better than sheds, but the best rural taverns had a tap room, a dining room, and a separate chamber or two—where beds were shared. Basic to tavern conviviality was the fact that their beer was 4 or 5 percent alcohol—much stronger than home-brew. Typical fare included bread and cheese, pigeon fricassee, roast fowl, pasties, and pies layered with apples, onions and cheese—washed down with a bowl of toddy or a mug of cider.

In 1704, Sara Knight traveled by horse from Boston to New York and back. Her diary complains of lean-to bedrooms resembling dog kennels, dirty pillows, bed ticks filled with corn husks, and bad food: "We would have eat a morsell, but the Pumpkin and Indian-mixt Bread had such an aspect, and the Bare-Legg'd Punch so awkerd or rather awfull that we left both."

Colonial Williamsburg boasts several taverns. Shields Tavern is reconstructed in the style of the 1745 original; its menu changes with the seasons, but may list peanut soup, ham simmered in root beer, bread pudding and peach cobbler. Christina Campbell's Tavern (1766) was frequented by George Washington; today, as then, it serves lump crab cakes and Gloucester chicken.

Goody Caldwell's Tavern in Ipswich, Massachusetts, served an extensive menu in the seventeenth century: Breakfast (about 7 a.m.): Suppawn, Johnny cake, sausages, eggs, doughnuts, and apple pie; Dinner dishes (2 p.m.): bean porridge, haunch of mutton, boiled beef and ham, boiled trout, baked beans

Bread was a colonial staple, baked in loaves of up to 8 pounds in weight. Since the dough contained no preservatives, it soon went stale. Dry bread was turned into crumbs in a mortar, and recycled in boiled puddings or other dishes.

Located on Duke of Gloucester Street in Colonial Williamsburg, the King's Arms reproduces the genteel chop house founded in 1772 by Jane Vobe. Its delectable Game Pye combines venison, rabbit and duck in a port wine sauce.

and pies; Supper (7 p.m.): calves' head soup, rump steak, meat pasties, head cheese, bubble and squeak and cold fowl.

The first major improvement to hearth cooking was the Rumford Fireplace, introduced in Britain and America in 1796. The Rumford design had angled sides to better reflect heat, a narrower chimney to reduce air turbulence, slow the consumption of logs and retain heat. The tin kitchen, a reflecting oven containing a spit and a dripping pan, was introduced about 1800; but the enclosed range was not introduced until 1815.

In wealthy households, especially in the South, the kitchen was a "dependency"—a separate structure. This "outdoor kitchen" reduced the danger of fire in the "big house" and kept ashes and cooking odors away from sensitive noses. Jefferson concealed his kitchens in Monticello's cellars; when he remodeled, he created eight separate brick cooking stations. These resembled brick closets in a row, each about 2 feet wide. The stations are open at the front, where the cook would stand. The fire is kindled on a shelf near the floor, and at the top is a round opening upon which the cooking pot sits.

Inventory of the Single Sisters House Kitchen, 1786

1 iron surface with 3 kettles set in
1 roasting oven with 2 plates and everything that goes with it
1 firedog
1 fire shovel and tongs
3 iron kettles
1 iron cooking pan
1 iron skimming spoon
2 tin kitchen spoons
1 small iron spoon
1 iron meat fork
1 kitchen cupboard
7 pewter soup bowls
1 pepper mill
1 tin strainer
2 tin funnels
1 tin grater
3 waterbuckets and a dipper
2 washing up tubs
3 vinegar kegs
1 old meat ax

This inventory of the Single Sisters Kitchen in the Moravian village of Old Salem includes culinary equipment improvements such as an iron cooking surface with three potholes, a roasting oven, and a tin grater.

IMPORTS AND EXPORTS

New foods affected not only diet and health but also trade, and trade between Old and New Worlds was significant. A letter of November 5, 1626 to the "High and Mighty Lords" controlling the West India Company, from their representative Pieter Schaghan, reported the arrival in Amsterdam of a ship from New Netherland with a cargo of 7,246 beaver skins, as well as the skins of otter, mink, lynx, and muskrat, plus nutwood and oak timbers.

Shortly after the founding of Boston, New England exported cattle, wool, tobacco and provisions to Virginia, Maryland and the West Indies as well as to Spain, Portugal and Britain. For beaver, moose and deer skins, England sent ironwares, horses, cheese, cotton and linen. Barbados traded in beef, pork, sugar, butter, salt, flour and indigo.

A cook pares and dices squash. Both squash and pumpkin were stewed—alone or with meat. They were dried for winter, and even used in cornmeal breads.

From 1645, New England vessels were sent to "the banks" for deep-water cod and mackerel. In 1665, 300 New England ships exported salted cod and mackerel to Malaga, the Canaries and the Portugal Islands. The colony also produced masts, timber, pitch, tar, pork, and corn. A new import at this time was the fork, introduced from the Continent.

Molasses, a byproduct of Caribbean sugarcane cultivation, began arriving at the Rhode Island colony by the late 1670s. In return, the colonists shipped to Barbados foods like pork, beef, butter, and cider.

Much of Virginia's wild ginseng headed for China, where it was considered a potent aphrodisiac.

By 1726, Charleston was exporting more than 4,000 tons of rice a year. At the same time, Carolinians and Virginians were importing pineapples from Barbados and 100-pound turtles from Jamaica.

Modern sweet corn, like this Merit variety, is chiefly yellow or white and yellow. Twenty-five percent of all modern supermarket goods contain corn.

While the average family bolted salt pork, beans, vegetables, and fish, the wealthy laid sumptuous tables with imported sugar, spices, raisins, almonds, figs and oranges. This dichotomy held true

in Jefferson's day. Monticello's larder was stocked with Parmesan cheese, anchovies, Italian olive oil and French mustard as well as wines from France, Portugal, Spain, Hungary, Germany and Italy.

But perhaps the most important import of all was the honeybee. America's first honeybees arrived in Jamestown in spring 1622, and, by the end of the seventeenth century, they had colonized much of the Atlantic coast.

Jefferson's beloved Monticello was never quite finished; a stickler for conveniences, he was always remodeling.

BEVERAGES

Cider was the colonies' chief beverage, commonly served at every meal. To whichever sleepyhead rose latest fell the difficult chore of drawing the day's cider from hogsheads in the cellar. Farms with extensive apple orchards usually boasted their own cider mills.

In addition to cider, the common man drank water, nut milk, tisanes of spruce needles, conserves dissolved in water, cherry bounce—brandy flavoured with fresh cherries—and meat broth. But as income increased, so did the variety of beverages consumed. Imported tea and coffee were poured in the parlor, and chocolate soon joined them.

The Olmecs had begun to cultivate chocolate trees 3,000 years ago. Christopher Columbus first recorded the Aztec name, *tchocolatl*, in 1502. Popular during Lent, chocolate was considered both a digestif and a restorative; French physicians used it to treat fevers and chest congestion.

The Baldwin was discovered as a chance seedling in Massachusetts in 1740. This heirloom apple variety was considered perfect both for eating out of hand and making cider. Photographed at Old Sturbridge Village.

While nuts and acorns are considered "hard mast," blueberries and other wild fruits like persimmons and fox grapes are called "soft mast." Both are enjoyed by foragers like bears and pigs.

Following the Boston Tea Party of 1773, patriots shunned imported, highly-taxed China tea for decoctions of domestic ingredients such as rose hips, chamomile, bergamot (Oswego tea) and pot marigold, as well as leaves of violets, blueberries and fireweed.

In the 1700s, the West India trade to the Atlantic coast brought rum—often accompanied by fresh limes. Artillery Punch, popular with both the military and civilians during this time, was based on tea, lemon and lime juice—and whatever spirits officers had in their flasks. New Englanders also began making their own rum, exporting it to West Africa on ships engaged in the slave trade.

Spirituous liquors were deemed suitable for reviving the fainting or warming the chilled, as well as for occasions like christenings, ordinations, Christmas and funerals. Brandy was distilled from local apples and peaches, and other tipples were imported—in considerable quantities.

The wealth of the palace's cellars at Williamsburg comes alive in the journal of John Fontaine, who joined Governor Alexander Spotswood in an expedition to the Blue Ridge Mountains: "September 6, 1716: We had a good dinner … and We drunk the Governor's health [in] … Virginia Red and White Wine, Irish Usquebaugh [whiskey], Brandy, Shrub, two sorts of Rum, champagne, Canary, Cherry punch, Cider, Water &c."

At Mount Vernon, George Washington poured apple brandy or rye whiskey for guests. Reconstructed in the twenty-first century, his distillery produces a limited-edition rye made from his personal recipe.

OTHER AMERICAN COLONIES

The food of other colonies gradually made its way across North America and was stirred into the great culinary melting pot.

For instance, in the Dutch colony of New Amsterdam, founded in 1624, bread was king. This foodstuff took the form of huge loaves, of stiff pancakes eaten out of the hand, of *poffertjes* (small pancakes), waffles, pretzels and *olie koecken* (precursors of the doughnut). Breakfast was typically bread with butter or cheese, a "sop" (bread soaked in vegetable broth), and a low-alcohol beer. The main meal consisted of a *hutspot* (a stew of vegetables with some meat), other meats and fruit. The evening meal was lighter: perhaps porridge, leftovers and more bread.

The local Munsee tribe had dined on succulent oysters for six thousand years, and Dutch colonists

followed suit. The newcomers imported cows and fruit trees from the Netherlands, but regularly consumed cornmeal mush, venison, turkey and ducks or striped bass or sturgeon from the Hudson. Even dolphin graced Dutch menus.

The entry for December 14, 1634, in the diary of Harmen Meyndertsz van den Bogaert, a surgeon with the Dutch West India Company, details daily fare: "We went out to shoot turkeys with the chief, but could not get any. In the evening I bought a very fat one for two hands of see-wan [wampum, a form of money consisting of strings or woven belts of shells]. The chief cooked it for us, and the grease he mixed with our beans and maize."

The Spanish territory of La Florida stretched from the Florida Keys to Newfoundland. Its first town was founded by Don Pedro Menendez de Airles in 1565 at the Timucan village of Seloy. Menendez named his capital St. Augustine—the first permanent European settlement in the New World. Many of his men married into the local tribe and grew accustomed to their cuisine.

Kitchen doors left open to allow breezes in also admitted thieves. Mr. Pug tries to carry away the "large and fat" turkey "upon the kitchen shelf," but the cook intercepts him and shakes him until he cannot bark.

The matrilineal Timucan cultivated the "three sisters"—corn, squash and beans (lima, string and shell). They gathered oysters, acorns, nuts, and the hearts of sabal palms. Spanish missions introduced barley, cabbage, cucumbers, figs, garlic, lettuce, oranges, peaches, and sugarcane as well as livestock. Florida proved unsuitable for cattle ranching, so the Spanish often ate alligator and manatee.

Although "American colonies" implies settlements on the Atlantic, the Spanish also settled in California and the American southwest. Missionaries planted figs, artichokes and citrus fruits in their walled gardens, and chilies; Mexican beans and cattle ranching spread through those regions.

After Vitus Bering's discovery of the Aleutians in 1741, Russian fur hunters gradually moved eastward to Alaska's mainland. The community of Kodiak supplied dried fish, dried yellow lily bulbs and blubber to other Russian settlements. Aleuts on the Aleutian Chain and the Alaska mainland began growing the potatoes and radishes introduced by their Russian conquerors. With the growing season too short for grain, the newcomers often ran out of bread. In 1805, for example, at the territorial capital of Sitka, the Russians dished up eagle, crow and cuttlefish.

Because Russia's Alaska settlements could not produce sufficient food and scurvy plagued residents, Ivan Kuskov of the Russian-American Company was directed to establish a colony in California. In March 1812 Kuskov chose a site on an isolated grassy bluff previously cultivated by local

A goat and two sheep respond to the dinner bell in the form of their mistress. Photographed at Hart's Square.

Native Americans. Carpenters building the redwood compound dined on blackberries, jackrabbits, black bear, and deer. Orchards were planted with four apple varieties, including Duchess of Oldenburg. Fenced fields were sown with wheat, barley and potatoes, while pigs fattened on mast.

Either the Russians or the Spanish introduced potatoes to the Makah, a native people of Washington state. That irregular tuber, also grown among the Tlingit, is today known as the Makah/Ozette.

Colonists who wished to grow crops were confronted with dense wilderness. Sixteenth-century potato patches were often surrounded by trees and brush that had not yet been cleared.

RECREATING COLONIAL FOOD TODAY

Both Hannah Glasse's 1760 *The Art of Cookery Made Plain and Easy* and a 1742 edition of Eliza Smith's 1727 *The Compleat Housewife* were sold in Williamsburg. However, the first cookbook to be written in North America was Amelia Simmons' *American Cookery*, printed in Connecticut in 1796. *American Cookery* stands out because it included the first recipes for "cramberry" sauce, pumpkin pie and Indian Pudding (a cornmeal mush enriched by stirring in eggs and milk, then baked).

This chicken and leek pie was seasoned with chopped fresh dill. Dill water (colonial "gripe water"), a tisane of dill seed, was given to babies suffering from colic.

APPLE TANSEY

Take three pippins, slice them round in thin slices, and fry them with butter; then beat four eggs, with six spoonfuls of cream, a little rosewater, nutmeg, and sugar; stir them together, and pour it over the apples; let it fry a little, and turn it with a pyre-plate. Garnish with lemon and sugar strew'd over it.

One of Eliza Smith's dessert recipes from *The Compleat Housewife*.

By featuring recipes for Indian Pudding, "Johnny Cake, or Hoe Cake," and Indian [corn] Slapjack, Simmons documents how central corn was to colonial diet. "Lightbread" was cornbread lavished with sugar and egg, with wheat flour substituted for a portion of the cornmeal.

Mrs. McLintock's Receipts for Cookery and Pastry-Work (1736) gives a recipe for Carrot Pudding—in McLintock's version, a very sweet dish.

CORN LIGHTBREAD

2 cups cornmeal
½ cup honey or sugar
½ teaspoon salt
1 cup all-purpose flour
2 teaspoons baking powder
2 cups buttermilk or sour milk
shortening size of an egg: melted lard, butter or bacon fat
1 beaten egg

Heat oven to 350 degrees. Heat and grease an iron skillet. Mix all dry ingredients and add melted shortening. Add buttermilk and egg; stir. Pour mixture into hot skillet. Bake about 45 minutes or until golden and tests done with toothpick inserted in middle. Ten servings.

New Netherland became New York in 1664. Language differences between the residents and their British overseers inspired the compiling of an English and Low-Dutch dictionary, published in 1730. Among Low-Dutch words still in use in American English are coleslaw, pickle and waffle.

The typical colonial cook depended on a manuscript cookbook—a hand-written guide passed down in families and amended as new recipes appeared on the horizon.

When William Penn set sail for the New World to escape religious tyranny, he packed "My Mother's Receipts for Cookerys Presarving and Chyrurgery."

Harriott Horry consulted such a receipt book at her Charleston home. A transcript was published in 1984: *A Colonial Plantation Cookbook: The Receipt Book of Harriot Pinckney Horry, 1770*. Receipts include a Carrot Pudding thickened with eight eggs and flavored with orange flower water.

A pot of beans simmers outdoors at the annual open house of Hart's Square, one man's collection of over ninety log structures including a grist mill, a communal oven, a tavern, and a print shop.

Martha Washington supervised the kitchen, larder, dairy, smokehouse, kitchen garden and dining rooms. Her cookbook was a small, leather-bound reference with recipes dating back to the sixteenth century. She began using it in 1749, and fifty years later gave it to her granddaughter, Eleanor Parke Custis. Among the 531 recipes was one for apple fritters.

The American Revolution Bicentennial in 1976 rekindled interest in preserving colonial dwellings and mastering hearth cooking. A spate of culinary history

Martha Washington's Great Cake was plump with raisins, ginger, mace, and almonds—all imported. Candied citron was prepared from citron melon. Leavened with forty egg whites, Great Cake was served at Christmas, New Year and on the anniversary of her wedding, January 6, 1759.

organizations were founded in the bicentennial's wake, and books with a new slant written. As a consequence, recreating colonial food is a simple matter of consulting collections of modernized recipes or browsing Internet sources.

At Colonial Williamsburg, Josiah Chowning's Tavern, whose painted sign bears a periwigged gent uncorking a bottle, serves Shepherd's Pie:

SHEPHERD'S PIE
Stew ingredients:
4 tablespoons melted butter
2 pounds lean boneless leg of lamb, cut into half-inch cubes
½ pound turnips, peeled and diced
½ pound carrots, peeled and diced
3 celery stalks, trimmed and sliced
1 medium onion, peeled and diced
1 teaspoon fresh thyme leaves
½ cup all-purpose flour
2 cups beef stock or water
⅓ cup tomato paste
salt and freshly ground black pepper to taste

Shepherd's Pie recipe continues on next page.

Potato topping:

2 pounds white or red boiling potatoes, peeled and diced into
  1-inch cubes

¼ pound unsalted butter

1 egg

1 egg yolk

1 teaspoon salt or to taste

½ teaspoon freshly ground white pepper or to taste

Stew: Melt the butter in a Dutch oven or large saucepan over medium high heat. Add lamb and brown on all sides, making sure not to crowd the pan. This may have to be done in batches. Remove the lamb from the pan with a slotted spoon and set aside.

Add turnips, carrots, celery and onion, and sauté for 3 minutes, stirring, or until onions are translucent. Return lamb to the pot with the thyme, and sprinkle flour over top. Cook over low heat for 3 minutes, stirring frequently, to cook the flour. Add the stock or water. Raise heat to medium high, and bring to a boil. Stir in tomato paste, and season with salt and pepper. Cook the lamb mixture covered over low heat for 40 to 55 minutes or until meat is tender.

Potato Topping: While lamb is braising, place the potatoes in salted cold water and bring to a boil. Boil until tender, about 15 minutes. Drain, and then mash with the butter, egg, yolk, salt and pepper. Place in a pastry bag fitted with a large star tip.

To serve, preheat oven broiler. Place the lamb in a large baking dish or individual dishes, and pipe the potatoes into a latticework on top. Place 6 inches below broiler element, and brown. Serve immediately. Serves 6 to 8.

At Colonial Williamsburg, a pedestrian in period costume strolls past homes, many of which have small family vegetable plots or herb gardens conveniently placed behind them.

In his coded diary kept from 1709 to 1712, William Byrd, owner of the Virginia plantation Westover, mentions dining on milk and chocolate for breakfast, on fish for dinner, and, during a visit to Williamsburg, French wine and beef. A social climber, Byrd was fussy about his wine and his ham.

TENNESSEE BOILED HAM

Wash ham well in cold water, and trim carefully. Soak overnight in cold water or half water and half milk. Place in kettle large enough with sufficient fresh water to cover ham entirely. Slowly bring to a boil. (This may take more than an hour.) Skim carefully, reduce heat, and simmer gently for 15 or 20 minutes to each pound. Cook until an ice pick inserted in the ham will reach the bone and no blood oozes when the pick is removed. The pick should be a little hard to extract; an overcooked ham will not slice well. Let the ham stay in the water until the water cools.

For a 10-pound smoked ham, add ½ cup brown sugar, ½ cup molasses and 1 teaspoon allspice to the boiling water.

Washington wrote to a friend, "My manner of living is plain ... A glass of wine and a bit of mutton is always ready..." He underplayed the fact that his home boasted two dining rooms, and a crew of African-American cooks, butlers and waiters. Meals featured hoe cakes, smoked ham, crab soup, apple fritters, puddings, tarts, cakes, and ice cream.

APPLE FRITTERS

1 egg
½ cup milk
1 tablespoon butter, melted
1 cup peeled, diced apple
1 cup sifted all-purpose flour
1 tablespoon sugar
1 teaspoon baking powder
¼ teaspoon salt
fat for deep frying
confectioners' sugar,
   optional

Heat fat to 375 degrees. Beat egg with milk. Stir in butter and apple. Combine dry ingredients; add to egg mixture and stir just until mixed. Drop from tablespoon into deep fat. Fry about four minutes, until brown outside and the inside is no longer doughy. Drain on paper toweling. Serve hot. If desired, roll in confectioners' sugar before serving. Makes sixteen.

Cold Crab Soup is most likely a descendant of the Scots' Partan Bree, which was served hot.

CRAB SOUP

½ cup chopped onion
¼ cup chopped celery and leaves
½ teaspoon anchovy paste, or 1 anchovy fillet
1 garlic clove, finely minced
2 tablespoons minced green bell pepper
¼ cup long-grain white rice
1 teaspoon minced fresh basil
¼ teaspoon white pepper
3 tablespoons butter
3 ripe tomatoes, peeled and chopped
1 bay leaf
1 cup chicken stock
1 cup fish stock or bottled clam juice
1 cup light cream
3 tablespoons dry sherry
1 cup minced cooked crab or she-crab
salt
crab legs or diced crab meat
fresh chives, minced

Sauté onion, celery, anchovy paste, garlic, bell pepper, rice, herbs and white pepper in butter 5 minutes, stirring constantly. Add tomato, bay leaf and chicken stock. Cover and cook over medium heat 30 minutes until vegetables and rice are tender. Discard bay leaf and puree mixture in blender. Combine puree with fish stock or clam juice, cream, sherry and minced crab. Heat without boiling; adjust seasoning. Cool, chill and again adjust seasoning to taste. Serve in chilled bowls garnished with crab legs or diced crab meat and sprinkled generously with chives. Four servings.

A guest at the President's House (now the White House) during Jefferson's tenure recorded a menu of "Rice soup, round of beef, turkey, mutton, ham, loin of veal, cutlets of mutton or veal, fried eggs, fried beef, a pie called macaroni... Ice cream very good" plus sweetmeats and fruit. Away from Washington, Jefferson partook chiefly of vegetables like asparagus

and ate salads year-round. Favorite dishes included muffins hot from the oven and white bean soup.

THE ARCHEOLOGICAL RECORD

Diaries and contemporary records do not always consider diet. Archeologists help to fill in the gaps.

Archeology has traced the roots of corn—one of the world's most important cereal grains. Grains of corn pollen 80,000 years old have been found in drill cores taken 200 feet below Mexico City. Corn was domesticated in Mesoamerica about 10,000 years ago, and its cultivation was central to Pre-Columbian societies. Bat caves in New Mexico have yielded tiny cobs 5,600 years old.

Above left: Dutch colonists were particularly fond of chives, a member of the onion family. Shaker cooks used the tender violet flowers to season omelets.

Above: Great northern beans, diced ham and fresh herbs will simmer to create white bean soup or "soup beans" as the dish is called in the American South.

Left: Viking settlers heated their domed homes with fire, which was also used to cook their meals. Mutton and fish were protein sources regularly consumed at the L'Anse aux Meadows site.

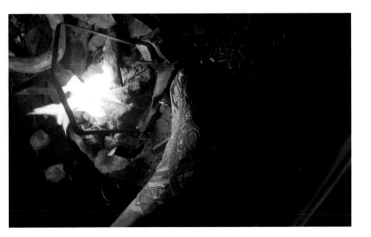

Archeological excavations at L'Anse aux Meadows in the 1960s uncovered the remains of three dwellings. When fierce winds blew off the Atlantic, their small herd of sheep could be sheltered in their four workshops or the iron-working smithy.

Discovered in 1960, the remains of eight Viking structures at L'Anse aux Meadows in Newfoundland prove that Vikings settled in North America a thousand years ago. Vikings began exploring west of Iceland as early as the tenth century, recording the temperate climate, timber, game, salmon, wild grapes and good pasture they discovered. Settlers at L'Anse aux Meadows lived in three wood-framed, peat-turf dwellings, with large cooking pits convenient to the largest structure. Remnants recovered include a woman's soapstone spindle whorl, indicating it is likely that they raised sheep, dined on mutton, and wore wool.

Wild "fox" grapes were the tasty variety found by early Norse explorers c. 1000, leading them to give the name "Vinland" to a northern area of North America—perhaps Newfoundland.

At Joara (near present-day Morganton, North Carolina), excavations of a burned hut in 2007 unearthed a Spanish iron scale and pottery sherds.

At St. Augustine, archeologists recovered amphora, trade beads, hawks bells and a dismembered donkey. Digs have led the Florida Museum of Natural History to conclude that the first American Thanksgiving was held on September 8, 1565, and that the menu was likely corn, fish, oysters, venison, garbanzos, hardtack, olives and wine.

At Jamestown, stores of beef and pork shipped from England were soon exhausted. Animal refuse from a 1610 pit proves that the primary foods were turtles and sea creatures like sturgeon and rays. The men and boys also consumed songbirds, oysters and raccoons. When starving, they cooked dogs, rats and poisonous snakes, and too often stooped to cannibalizing corpses.

Digs at Strawbery Banke have yielded objects of ceramic, glass, metal, wood, bone, shell and leather, as well as seeds and remains of meals—more than 700,000 specimens covering 300 years of urban New Hampshire history.

A Mount Vernon midden dating from the early years of George and Martha's marriage has proved very fruitful, according to Director of Archeology Esther C. White. Among the 75,000 items recovered were wine bottles, oyster shells and crab claws, as well as seeds and animal bones, most deposited between 1750 and 1775. Beneath a major slave dwelling, the House of Families, 25,000 animal remains came to light including duck, deer, squirrel and rabbit.

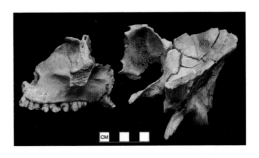

Pig cranial bones excavated from the South Grove Midden at Mount Vernon document some of the food eaten at Mount Vernon between 1750 and 1775.

Remains of meals excavated at Joara prove that this Native American mound-builders' settlement cultivated large corn fields in the nearby bottomland. Spanish expeditions led by Hernando de Soto (1540) and Juan Pardo (1567–8) paused here while seeking an overland route to Mexico.

PLACES TO VISIT

America has a wealth of restored or replicated colonial sites such as Old Sturbridge Village, Historic Deerfield, the Museum of American Frontier Culture (Staunton, Virginia), the Museum of Appalachia (a Smithsonian affiliate in Tennessee), the Stanley-Whitman House (Connecticut), Baltimore City Life Museum, Missouri Town (Blue Springs, Missouri), Colonial Williamsburg and the Ontario Historical Society (Willowdale, Ontario). Below are listed just a sampling. Many of these sites are peopled with costumed interpreters/re-enactors.

Three women take a breather behind a spacious cabin at Colonial Williamsburg. Piles of firewood season nearby.

"Free-range" chickens were the only kind known in the colonies. Geese served as alarm bells, warning of approaching strangers.

The Claude Moore Colonial Farm, 6310 Georgetown Pike, McLean, Virginia. Website: www.1771.org

Virginia's Claude Moore Colonial Farm is a living history museum portraying life on a small, low-income, tenant farm just before the Revolutionary War. Visitors stroll a walking path through wheat and corn fields and an orchard to access the farmhouse. Special events include fairs, as well as cheese-making and flax-processing demonstrations. Cattle, turkeys, hogs, chickens, friendly dogs and cats delight young visitors.

Two costumed interpreters at Plimoth Plantation prepare to use a communal beehive oven to bake their round breads. The woman at the rear inserts loaves with a wooden peel.

The Colonial Pennsylvania Plantation, Ridley Creek State Park, Media,
   Pennsylvania. Website: www.colonialplantation.org
   New to the pantheon, the Colonial Pennsylvania Plantation was begun
   in 1973. It exhibits the period 1720 to 1820 when the Pratt Family was
   in residence. The farmer in residence tills fields, fashions tools or cares
   for livestock. Visiting children have a choice of cooking over an open
   hearth or molding candles. Typical events include a French and Indian
   War skirmish, a ghost tour, or digging at an archeological site. Open
   weekends or holidays only.

Colonial Spanish Quarter Living History Museum, 29 St. George Street,
   St. Augustine, Florida. Website: www.historicstaugustine.com

When the Andres Ximenez's house was built in 1798, the kitchen was assigned a separate structure. This building was constructed of coquina or tabby, a mixture of limestone and shells. The large cast-iron pot was used for laundry.

Colonial Spanish Quarter Living History Museum is a two-block
institution replicating a Spanish outpost, a 1740s garrison town.
Feel free to chat with the blacksmith, candle maker, and carpenter
or a soldier and his wife. Sample period
food and drink at the Taberna del Gallo.
The Ximenez-Fatio House Museum is
located nearby on Cadiz Street.

Colonial Williamsburg has researched heritage breeds of livestock and domestic fowl, and examples are seen grazing in fenced pastures throughout the grounds.

Colonial Williamsburg, 101 S. Henry Street,
   Williamsburg, Virginia. Website:
   www.colonialwilliamsburg.com
   Restoring the city of Williamsburg to its

eighteenth-century appearance was the lifelong dream of William Goodwin, twice rector of Bruton Parish Church (1660). Goodwin convinced John D. Rockefeller Jr. to fund the project; restoration began in 1926 and continued through the 1930s. More than 300 buildings had to be torn down or moved, and others totally reconstructed. Today's visitors can watch glassblowers, blacksmiths and other artisans produce goods via colonial methods. A recent addition is a farm with a corncrib, slave dwelling and other outbuildings. Taverns offer period food.

Davenport Colonial Homestead, Mt. Tabor Road, Creswell, North Carolina. Website: www.stamfordhistory.org/dav_homestead.htm

Davenport Colonial Homestead is a modest late-eighteenth-century farm consisting of a home and a loom house. Built by Daniel Davenport, the county's first senator, the main dwelling (1776) measures less than 600 square feet.

Historic Deerfield, Old Main Street, Deerfield, Massachusetts. Website: www.historic-deerfield.org
Historic Deerfield is an open-air living history museum centered around eleven house museums lining the original, mile-long street. Site of one of the last

A bean vine climbs a wooden "teepee" in an eighteenth-century-style vegetable garden.

Native American raids in New England, Historic Deerfield is dedicated to early colonial life in the Connecticut River Valley.

Jamestown Settlement, 2110 Jamestown Road, Williamsburg, Virginia. Telephone 888 593 4682. Website: www.historyisfun.org/Jamestown-Settlement.htm
Jamestown Settlement features a recreated Powhatan Indian village, a colonial fort, and replicas of the three ships that brought English settlers to the New World in 1607. A 30,000-square foot museum displays period artifacts. Hands-on activities include scraping animal hides, grinding corn, donning armor, steering a ship, and squeezing into a sailor's bunk. Its mission is to tell the story of the three cultures (European, Native American and African) that came together here "to lay the foundation for a uniquely American form of democratic government, language, free enterprise and society." Food items are available at www.shophistoryisfun.com. Jamestown Settlement is within a thirty-minute drive of the Yorktown Victory Center.

Mount Vernon, 3200 Mt. Vernon Memorial
    Highway, Mount Vernon, Virginia.
    www.mountvernon.org
    The Washingtons called Mount Vernon
    home for more than forty years.
    The Mount Vernon Ladies' Association
    purchased the neglected property in
    1858 and have combined research and
    archeology to reconstruct its history.
    The mansion has been restored to look
    as it did in 1799. The grounds include Washington's tomb, a 4-acre
    demonstration farm and a reconstructed slave cabin as well as a
    museum, theaters, and galleries.

After plowing
their fields,
colonial farmers
broadcast seed for
wheat, oats, rye or
barley by hand.

Mulford Farm, 10 James Lane, East Hampton, New York.
    www.easthamptonhistory.org/museums.php
    An intact English colonial farmstead—one of the best in the nation.
    Open Memorial Day through
    Columbus Day weekend. The site
    includes the farmhouse (1680),
    barn (1720), spinning dependency,
    privy, smokehouse, and garden.

A root cellar dug
into a hill helped
to preserve
vegetables like
turnips, cabbages,
onions and carrots
with its cool
temperatures.
Photographed
at the Museum
of Appalachia.

Museum of Appalachia, 2819 Andersonville
    Highway, Clinton, Tennessee. Website:
    www.museumofappalachia.org
    Founded by John Rice Irwin, the
    50-acre Museum of Appalachia site
    displays thirty authentic structures
    plus exhibits of 400,000 frontier
    items, many of them farming tools and
    implements. Look for cabins that have
    been used in films as well as newborn
    lambs in spring, a July Fourth anvil
    shoot, and a Fall Homecoming with
    Mountain Music. The cafe serves stew
    beans and cornbread.

The New Hampshire Farm Museum, 1305
    White Mountain Highway, Milton,
    New Hampshire. Website:
    www.farmmuseum.org

When not supervising their large plantations, men like George Washington and Thomas Jefferson enjoyed visiting Virginia's colonial capital, Williamsburg, discussing politics and dining at the taverns there.

The New Hampshire Farm Museum (est. 1979) consists of two adjoining farmsteads on 50 acres. The Jones home is a microcosm of house styles, extended from the 1770s to the early 1900s. Other buildings include a three-storey Great Barn housing a collection of farm tools, the John York Cider Mill, and a blacksmith shop. Attractions include summer vegetable gardens, winter sleigh rides, forest hiking trails, and a carriage display.

Old Salem Museums & Gardens, 600 S. Main Street, Winston-Salem, North Carolina. Website: www.oldsalem.org
Established in 1950, Old Salem recreates a historic Moravian town in the period 1766–1840, with original buildings plus several modern museums and a spacious visitors' center. Winkler Bakery (1800) is the oldest continually operating bakery in North Carolina, complete with wood-fired brick bake ovens and hand-mixed dough for cookies and other sweets. The remains of an earlier Moravian settlement, Bethabara, are a short drive away.

Old Sturbridge Village, 1 Old Sturbridge Road, Sturbridge, Massachusetts. Website: www.osv.org
Opened in 1946, Old Sturbridge Village is New England's largest pioneer village, covering 200 acres. Depending on the season, events

may include plowing, an heirloom plant sale, carding and spinning, apple picking, or stagecoach rides. Sheep are sheared on Memorial Day. Blacksmiths, coopers and potters ply their trades. Muster Day is especially enjoyable for children.

Plimoth Plantation, 137 Warren Avenue, Plymouth, Massachusetts. Website: www.plimoth.org
Plimoth Plantation replicates the village of Plimoth in 1627, seven years after the Pilgrims arrived and just as colonists began to disperse into neighboring territory. Compact houses are surrounded by an 8-foot-tall paling. Interpreters readily answer questions about gardening, parenting, education, religion, cooking, housekeeping, and relations with the Wampanoag. Nearby are a Pilgrim graveyard and the *Mayflower II* (a full-scale replica donated in 1957 by the people of Great Britain).

Historic St. Mary's City, P.O. Box 39, St. Mary's City, Maryland. Website: www.stmaryscity.org
St. Mary's is the fourth-oldest British settlement in North America and was Maryland's first capital. This open-air museum portrays seventeenth-century life prior to and during Maryland's colonization. Hearth cooking, butchering, preserving, dairying, dyeing, and medicinal practices are demonstrated.

The small Moravian community of Bethabara was settled in 1753 by colonists from Pennsylvania. At this remote site in North Carolina, a stockade helped to keep bears, wolves, unfriendly natives and outlaws at bay.

Strawbery Banke, 14 Hancock Street, Portsmouth, New Hampshire.

Website: www.strawberybanke.org

Strawbery Banke is a 10-acre museum tracing nearly three centuries in one of America's oldest continuously occupied neighborhoods,

A costumed couple works together on raised garden beds at Plimoth Plantation in Massachusetts.

Puddle Dock. The site features restored houses (the oldest dates to 1695), shops and period gardens. An inn occupies a house built before 1814. Open May through October. Call ahead regarding cooking and gardening workshops.

Colonial Wormsloe, 7601 Skidaway Road, Savannah, Georgia. Website: www.gastateparks.org/Wormsloe Colonial Wormsloe is the estate of Noble Jones, a carpenter who reached America in 1733. His home's tabby (tabby, or coquina, is a building material of ground seashells, lime, sand and salt water) ruins comprise the oldest standing structure in Georgia. Jones served the colony as doctor, constable, Indian agent and surveyor. A museum with artifacts from the site is featured. Events include music, dancing, a muster, cannon firing, demonstrations of woodworking, blacksmithing, cooking, spinning, flint knapping, leatherwork, and pewter casting, depending on the season.

FURTHER READING

In colonial Maryland, a settler wrote, "Wee cannot sett down a foote but tred on strawberries." Native Americans mixed crushed wild strawberries with cornmeal for bread.

Andrews, William L. (ed.). *Six Women's Slave Narratives*. With a Foreword by Henry Louis Gates, Jr. New York/Oxford: Oxford University Press, 1988.

Bullock, Helen. *The Williamsburg Art of Cookery or, Accomplish'd Gentlewoman's Companion: Being a Collection of upwards of Five Hundred of the most Ancient & Approv'd Recipes in Virginia Cookery*. Richmond, Virginia: Colonial Williamsburg, 2007.

Craughead, Thomas. *Thomas Jefferson's Crème Brulee: How a Founding Father and his Slave James Hemings Introduced French Cuisine to America*. Philadelphia: Quick Books, 2012.

Divina, Fernando and Marlene and the Smithsonian National Museum of the American Indian. *Foods of the Americas: Native Recipes and Traditions*. Berkeley/Toronto: Ten Speed Press, 2004.

Farb, Peter and George Armelagos. *Consuming Passions: The Anthropology of Eating*. Boston: Houghton Mifflin, 1980.

Gunderson, Mary. *Cooking on the Lewis and Clark Expedition*. Mankato, Minnesota: Blue Earth Books, 2000.

Library of Congress American Memory website. Contains original documents, maps, slave narratives, details about immigration and transportation; teachers' resources. www.memory.loc.gov.

Oliver, Sandra L. *Food in Colonial and Federal America*. Westport, CT: Greenwood Press, 2005.

Penner, Lucille Recht. *Eating the Plates: A Pilgrim Book of Food and Manners*. New York: Macmillan Publishing Company, 1991.

Simmons, Amelia. *American Cookery 1796*. Introduction and Updated Recipes by Iris Ihde Frey. Green Farms, Connecticut: The Silverleaf Press, 1984.

Stavely, Keith and Fitzgerald, Kathleen. *America's Founding Food: The Story of New England Cooking*. Chapel Hill, North Carolina: The University of North Carolina Press, 2004.

BIBLIOGRAPHY

Adams, James Ring. "1609: The Year Everything Changed," *National Museum of the American Indian magazine*. Washington, DC: National Museum of the American Indian, Spring 2009.

Aller, Joan E. *Cider Beans, Wild Greens, and Dandelion Jelly*. Kansas: Andrews McMeel Publishing, 2010.

Bryan, Mollie. "Spoon bread carries history of good taste," in *Relish magazine, The Augusta Chronicle*, Augusta, Georgia, October 15, 2008.

Bullock, Helen. *The Williamsburg Art of Cookery or Accomplished Gentlewoman's Companion*. Richmond, Virginia: The Dietz Press for Colonial Williamsburg, 2007.

Carpenter, Teresa (ed.). *New York Diaries: 1609 to 2009*. New York: Modern Library, 2012.

Costain, Thomas B. *The White and the Gold: The French Regime in Canada*. Toronto: Doubleday Canada Limited, 1954.

Crews, Ed. "Colonial Foodways," *Colonial Williamsburg Journal*, Autumn 2004.

Daley, Bill. "Columbus' Historic Voyages Changed the World's Menu," *Chicago Tribune*, October 8, 2008.

Dow, George F. *Every Day Life in the Massachusetts Bay Colony*. 1935. Reissued New York: Dover Publications, Inc., 1988.

Frey, Iris Ihde (ed.). *American Cookery, 1796, by Amelia Simmons*. Green Farms, Connecticut: The Silverleaf Press, 1984.

Gauquier, Anthony. *Pilgrim Recipes: The food that kept them alive the first winter*. Bridgewater, Massachusetts: Castelot-Ferreira, 1980.

George, Jean Craighead. *Acorn Pancakes, Dandelion Salad and 38 Other Wild Recipes*. New York: HarperCollins, 1995.

Glasse, Henry. *Pattern in the Material Folk Culture of the Eastern United States*. Philadelphia: University of Pennsylvania Press, 1968.

Gollner, Adam L. *The Fruit Hunters*. New York: Scribner, 2008.

Harris, John. *Saga of the Pilgrims: From Europe to the New World*. Chester, Connecticut: The Globe Pequot Press, 1990.

Heath, Dwight B. (ed.). *Mourt's Relation: A Journal of the Pilgrims at Plymouth*. From the original text of 1622. Boston: Applewood Books, 1986.

Katz, William Loren. *Eyewitness: The Negro in American History*. New York: Pittman Publishing, 1971.

Kaufman, Frederick. *A Short History of the American Stomach*. New York: Harcourt, Inc., 2008.

LeFever, Gregory. "Early Cooking Hearths." *Early American Life*. Shaker Heights, Ohio. October 2009.

McLeod, Stephen A. (ed.). *Dining With the Washingtons: Historic Recipes, Entertaining and Hospitality from Mount Vernon*. University of North Carolina Press, 2011.

Moser, Laura. "All the President's Produce," *The Wall Street Journal*, April 28–29, 2012, D-9.

The Museum of the Concord Antiquarian Society. *An Olde Concord Christmas*. New York: St. Martin's Press, 1980.

Raver, Anne. "Totally Green Apples," *The New York Times*, November 17, 2011, D-1, D-6.

Roberts, Sam. "A History of New York in 50 Objects," *The New York Times*, September 2, 2012, 24–26.

Rolland, Jacques L., Sherman, Carol, et al. *The Food Encyclopedia*. Toronto, Ontario: Robert Rose Inc., 2006.

Sherman, Sandra. *Fresh From the Past: Recipes and Revelations from Moll Flanders' Kitchen*. New York: Taylor Trade Publishing, 2004.

Theobald, Mary Miley. "Sampling 18th-Century Fare at Shields Tavern," *Colonial Williamsburg Journal*, Winter 1992–3.

Tortorello, Michael. "In Praise of the Misunderstood Quince," *The New York Times*, May 3, 2012, D-1, D-2.

INDEX

2009

To my dear friend, Connie who has a heart
of gold, a zest for life and a love of
critters.

Love,
Valerie